ONCE IT CLICKS, THERE'S NO GOING BACK.

MS CAT

ONCE IT CLICKS, THERE'S NO GOING BACK.

CONTENTS

DEDICATION

First and foremost, I give all honor and thanks to the Most High. Thank you for the gift, the calling, and the talent I didn't even realize I possessed. Thank you for trusting me with a voice, a vision, and an assignment that at times felt heavier than I thought I could carry. This book exists because You saw something in me long before I ever saw it in myself.

I dedicate this book to my father, Johnny Mitchell. Although I didn't get the opportunity to spend as much time with you as I would have wanted, I know without question that your DNA lives inside of me. Your hustle runs through my blood and pulses through my veins. In many ways, that hustle fuels me even now. I feel your presence in the way I move, the way I think, and the way I refuse to quit. When I'm tired, when I'm unsure, when the road feels lonely, I feel your strength pushing me forward. I know you're looking down on me, and I hope you're proud because everything I am becoming is rooted in who you were.

I also dedicate this book to my grandmother, Lucille. You always told me I was special, even when I didn't believe it, even when I couldn't see it, even when life tried to convince me otherwise. Now, I'm finally starting to understand what you saw all along. I carry your words with me, and I carry your love with me. I hope I am honoring you in the way I show up, the way I lead, and the way I leave a mark.

This book is dedicated to my daughters, Shealtiel Cannon and Liora Knowles. You guys have walked this journey with me through the trenches, through the highs, the lows, the uncertainty, the wins, and the losses. You both have seen me when things were good and stood by me when things were hard. You two are the reason I live, the reason I move, and the reason I have my being. If it had not been for you guys, I don't know if I would have found the strength to become the hustler, the grinder, and the woman I am today. Thank you for choosing me. Thank you for giving me purpose beyond myself.

I dedicate this book to everyone who has played a role in my journey. Some are still in my life. Some are not. Out of respect, I will leave names unspoken, because some stories are better left untold. But know this: if you helped me in any capacity, if you opened a door, offered guidance, gave encouragement, or stood beside me when I was building my first office, my first business, or my first belief in myself, this book is for you, too. I am grateful for every lesson, every assist, and every moment that shaped me into who I am becoming.

Finally, I dedicate this book to you, the dreamer. To the one wondering if entrepreneurship is really for you. To the one whose family tells them to "just get a job." To the one who feels misunderstood, out of place, or like the minority in every room they walk into. To the one who knows there is more inside of them, even if no one else sees it yet. *This book is for you.*

Crack it open with an open mind and an open heart. Know that you are not alone on this path. Know that someone else has walked it, stumbled on it, doubted themselves on it, and kept going anyway. Thank you for taking this journey with me.

WHO THIS BOOK IS FOR

This book is for you if you've ever looked at someone close to you and thought, *Wait... they were just like me.* They had a regular nine-to-five. A regular life. Regular pressures. And one day, something *clicked*. They decided they didn't want their time, their energy, or their income controlled by anyone else. They decided to make money with their own two hands and you watched that journey unfold. And somewhere along the way, you asked yourself: *Could that be me?*

Maybe you're scared. Maybe you have an idea but don't know if it's good enough. Maybe you don't know if *you're* good enough. Maybe you've been hustling your whole life, but nothing about it feels legit yet. No real structure. No real brand. Just grind. If that sounds like you, this book was written with you in mind. This book is for you because it's from you. Not from someone who started on third base. Not from someone born into opportunity. Not from someone selling a fantasy. It's from the person who got it out of the mud. From the person who was working a nine-to-five, got fired, bounced from couch to couch, hustled, struggled, and kept trying to figure out a way forward.

It hasn't always been pretty. It hasn't always been comfortable. And it definitely hasn't always been rainbows, butterflies, and feel-good moments. But it has always been real. I'm not writing this as someone looking down. I'm writing this as someone who stood exactly where you're standing and made a decision, *not because it was easy, but because it was necessary.* I'm the voice of the regular person who finally clicked. So if something inside you is waking up...if you're tired of playing small...if you're ready to stop watching other people live the life you want... this book is for you. And if you're ready to

CLICK, you're exactly where you're supposed to be.

How It Clicked

I didn't sit down one day and decide to create a framework. *CLICK* wasn't something I mapped out on a whiteboard or pulled from a workbook. I lived it long before I ever gave it a name. Looking back, I can see exactly how the pattern kept repeating itself in my life, every time I leveled up, every time I survived something I thought would break me, every time I became someone new. That pattern is what you're about to read. At different points in my journey, I needed different things. Sometimes I needed clarity. Sometimes I needed courage. Sometimes I just needed to keep going when quitting felt easier. What I didn't realize at the time is that every transition followed the same rhythm.

Things would *click*. Not all at once. Not overnight. But internally. That quiet moment when something shifts inside you and you realize you can't unsee the truth anymore. The moment where staying the same feels heavier than changing. The moment where excuses stop working. That's what this book is built around.

CLICK represents the internal progression I went through—not as steps to memorize, but as phases you *recognize*.

Clarity came when I realized the life I was living no longer fit who I was becoming.

Leverage showed up when I used what I already had instead of waiting for what I didn't.

Implementation happened the moment I stopped thinking and started moving.

Confidence was built by repetition, not perfection.

Keep Going became the real test because motivation fades, but purpose doesn't.

You'll notice something important as you read: *I'm not telling you what to do. I'm showing you what happened.* Each chapter reflects a season of my life where something broke open—mentally, emotionally, spiritually—and forced me to grow. And my hope is that as you read, you'll start recognizing yourself in these moments. Because **CLICK** isn't about business mechanics. It's about decision points. It's about the moment you stop playing the role and start becoming it. It's about choosing progression over comfort. Wanting more doesn't mean something is wrong with you. It simply means you're ready for what's next.

You don't need to read this book looking for instructions. You don't need to finish it feeling pressured. All I ask is that you read it honestly. Pay attention to what resonates. Notice what makes you uncomfortable. Listen for what keeps tapping you on the shoulder. If something clicks for you, that's not a coincidence. That's alignment. And by the time you finish this book, my hope is simple: You won't be asking *if* you're

ready anymore. You'll know.

CLARITY

Ten years ago, I was a mother to a four-year-old and a seven-year-old, and property management had already become my life. When my youngest was born, I was already in the industry. I started as a leasing agent, bounced from property to property, and worked my way up the ladder the only way I knew how: *by showing up, staying late,* and doing whatever it took to be the best. Eventually, that grind paid off. I was offered a position at one of the largest properties in

Houston, and if you know anything about property management, you know this: the larger the property, the bigger the paycheck.

I had just turned thirty. I was young, ambitious, and making more money than I ever had before. I thought I had made it. I thought this was success. At that point, my leasing team and I were the highest paid in the industry. My boss was phenomenal, and I respected her deeply. She was sharp, disciplined, and ran a tight ship. She only had one non-negotiable rule: *I had to be in my office every single day.* No exceptions. That meant missed recitals. Missed extracurricular activities. Missed moments I knew I could never get back. Work wasn't just important. It was everything. But in exchange, my girls had a good life. We moved out of the hood and into a nice place. My daughters were enrolled in a great childcare program. Money was flowing. Bills were paid. On paper, I was set—a good salary, benefits, a stable career path. From the outside, people would have said, *"She's doing well."* And in many ways, I was. My children were taken care of. I was providing. Financially, I showed up. But here's the truth: *I wasn't free.* I was chained to a job that demanded my life. I was always on call, dropping everything when work called. That level of commitment takes a toll—physically, mentally, emotionally—but at the time, I didn't question it.

As a mother, I lived inside a trade-off no one ever said out loud: time or money. In that season, money won. Not because I didn't care—but because I felt I had no choice. I showed up no matter what. Sick days didn't exist. Exhaustion wasn't an excuse. I kept going, convinced that consistency would eventually be rewarded and that sacrifice would be recognized. I gave them everything, believing loyalty meant something... until the day it didn't.

Before entrepreneurship, I was comfortable. I held down the six-figure role as a property manager overseeing that 1,500-unit complex—which essentially was a small city. I led a team of more than a hundred people: maintenance crews, leasing agents, and office managers. The work was demanding, relentless, and all-consuming. And because it consumed my life, my relationships became intertwined with it.

My team wasn't just a staff—it felt like family. To me, leadership was personal. It was about people, not position. We spent long days together, shared real conversations, and supported one another beyond the job description. I believed that level of commitment meant something. I believed it created security.

Then the property was sold. And just like that, more than a hundred of us were gone. No warning. No thank you. *No loyalty returned.* I remember that day like it was yesterday. The silence in the office was deafening. Normally, there would be phones ringing, radios chirping, people moving in and out, constant noise, constant motion. That day, everything was still. Too still. A hundred lives standing on the edge of something none of us had prepared for. When it hit me, it wasn't gradual. It felt like someone had punched me in the throat. My chest tightened instantly, and I was gasping for air, the kind of gasp where your body forgets how to breathe. Like when you're drinking something too fast, and it goes down the wrong pipe, and you're choking, gagging, struggling just to catch your breath. That's what it felt like. I couldn't speak. I couldn't think clearly. My body reacted before my mind could make sense of what was happening. Everything I had built, everything I had given myself to, disappeared in a single moment. And in that silence, standing there trying to breathe, I realized how quickly stability can vanish.

At first, I was stunned. I couldn't even process it. Then the anger hit. Because this wasn't just a job. They had taken my time, my loyalty, my sacrifices. They robbed me of moments with my kids I could never get back. And after all that, they tossed me aside like it was nothing. That anger turned into clarity: *Never again*. Never again would I put myself in a position where someone else decided my worth. Never again would I give someone else the authority to dictate whether I could provide for my family. That day, something in me snapped awake.

The day I lost my job was the day I found my freedom. But clarity doesn't always mean the path forward is smooth. My next move wasn't straight into millions. It was missteps, trial and error, and figuring things out the hard way. I dabbled in film and production. I was chasing a dream, and for a moment, it looked like I was catching it. One of my biggest accomplishments was directing my first feature film, and we landed a full premiere at AMC 30 Dunvale. Hundreds of people lined up. A red carpet rolled out. The buzz in the air was undeniable. PR cameras flashing. My name on the marquee as

Director. People congratulated me as if I had made it.

For those couple of hours, I let myself feel it. The pride. The applause. The dream. But here's the part nobody saw. I barely had enough money to scrape together an outfit for my own premiere. And when the credits rolled, when the lights came up, and the crowd filed out, my team was digging for gas money just to get home. That was the moment it hit me. The difference between looking successful and actually being successful. On the outside, it looked like I had arrived. On the inside, I was starving. That contrast cut deep. I couldn't keep living in a façade, shining for the cameras but broke in reality. I wanted more than the highlight reel. I wanted the real thing. That was the first real moment of clarity for me.

CLARITY CAME WHEN I REALIZED I DIDN'T WANT TO PLAY THE ROLE ANYMORE. I WANTED TO BE THE ROLE. I WANTED TO BE THE PERSON EVERYONE ALREADY PERCEIVED ME TO BE, AND I WANTED MY BANK ACCOUNT TO MATCH. I WAS TIRED OF BEING A STARVING ARTIST.

REFLECTION:

CLARITY

Before you move forward, pause. If you've felt a nudge to shift, a quiet pull telling you that where you are isn't where you're meant to stay, don't disregard it. That feeling isn't random, and it isn't selfish. It's awareness. A lot of people ignore that nudge because it comes wrapped in guilt. Guilt for wanting more. Guilt for questioning a life that looks "good enough." Guilt for feeling restless when nothing is technically wrong. But clarity doesn't always arrive as certainty. Sometimes it shows up as discomfort. As restlessness. As a quiet knowing that the life you're living no longer fits who you're becoming. That doesn't mean you're ungrateful. It means you're evolving.

You can appreciate what a season gave you and still recognize when it's time to move on. Growth often feels like tension before it feels like peace. And just because you don't have all the answers yet doesn't mean the question is invalid.

If you're here, reading this, something already resonated. Something already stirred. And instead of judging that feeling or pushing it down, this is your moment to acknowledge it. Not to rush. Not to decide everything today. Just to be honest with yourself.

So take a moment and reflect:

What part of my life feels misaligned

right now?

_____

_____

_____

_____

_____

_____

_____

_____

_____

_____

_____

_____

_____

_____

_____

_____

_____

Where have I been ignoring my own truth because it felt safer to stay put?

_____

_____

_____

_____

_____

_____

_____

_____

_____

_____

_____

_____

_____

_____

_____

_____

If nothing changed in the next year,

how would that make me feel?

_____

_____

_____

_____

_____

_____

_____

_____

_____

_____

_____

_____

_____

_____

_____

_____

Clarity isn't about having the perfect plan. It's about being honest enough to admit when something isn't working anymore. The version of you who wants more isn't ungrateful. They're aware. And awareness is always the first shift. Sit with that, because once clarity hits, the role you've been playing starts to crack.

CEO MODE ACTIVATED.

LEVERAGE

When I signed the lease to my first office, I was nervous as hell. I didn't have money like that. I didn't have a safety net. I didn't have investors lined up. Truth be told, I didn't even have a pot to piss in.

WHAT I DID HAVE WAS A DECISION I HAD ALREADY MADE: FAILURE WAS NOT AN OPTION ANYMORE.

And failure, to me, was very clear. Failure was living from pillow to post, bouncing from my ex-boyfriend's house to my mama's house just to have somewhere to sleep. Failure was not being able to provide for my kids. Failure was not being able to stand on my own two feet. Failure was going backward to a life I had already mentally outgrown. I could not fail. That understanding became my fuel. When I looked at my kids, I reminded myself that working for someone else had once allowed me to earn six figures. If I could do it for them, why couldn't I do it for myself?

When the realtor slid the paperwork across the desk, I remember thinking, *this is it.* There was no turning back. They gave me three months free, and while that sounded like a blessing, it also felt like a countdown. I felt the fear and kept going.

Having a physical location was one of the scariest things I had ever done, but it also kept me focused. Walking into that 2,300-square-foot office every day was a reality check. It reminded me what I was building and what was at stake. Looking back, I don't know if I would have made it if I had tried to do it virtually at that time.

That space grounded me. Those three months became my runway. Night and day, day and night, I was in that office building, making something out of nothing. No staff. No blueprint. Just vision.

Before starting my own firm, I had worked one tax season with a colleague, helping her launch her tax business from scratch. Everything I learned during that time, everything she taught me, and everything we learned from her mentor, I applied directly to building my own office. I poured it into building something of my own. I pulled from every place I could. I used my experience from property management—the systems, the structure, the discipline. I pulled from lessons I learned in the film industry. I took every piece of wisdom, every life lesson, every bit of knowledge I had access to and tried to make it work for me. I went old school. Pen to paper. Organizing ideas in notebooks. Spreadsheets. Checklists. A whiteboard filled with plans, reminders, and things I needed to figure out. I was figuring it out as I went, relying on what I already knew and what I could research and apply. I built with what I had.

What anchored me through that season was my faith in the Most

High and the promise I made to myself. A promise that I would never turn back. A promise that I would never let anyone control my destiny or my pockets again. And an unspoken promise I made to my kids—that I would be a stable parent, whether I was in a relationship or not. That I would be consistent. That I would provide.

Sometimes you have to motivate yourself. Sometimes you have to set small milestones and reward yourself along the way. But staying focused, staying grounded in faith, and keeping my eyes on what mattered. That's what got me through. I put ads on Indeed and started meeting complete strangers. Real conversations. I told them straight up: *"I'm starting this from scratch. I don't have all the answers yet, but I need good people who are willing to build with me."* Some said no. Some fell off. But some stayed. And the ones who stayed mattered. A lot of them were willing to work on commission only. That alone told me something. It wasn't about the paycheck. It was about the vision. Looking back, I can see how intentional God was. Even in my uncertainty, He kept sending the right people at the right time. Not all of them were vision carriers. Not all of them were permanent. But all of them were necessary. When Flat Fee was brand new, and nobody knew who I was, God sent me foot soldiers. People willing to get out, pass out flyers, market, and spread the word about Flat Fee Tax Prep & Services. A lot of them never completed a single tax return. Some didn't even make it that far. But they served the purpose they were meant to serve. When I needed structure, I had people step up as managers. When I needed support, I had individuals working Flat Fee on the side. I had people working in the office who quit their jobs to be there, even when I couldn't pay them upfront.

As I continued moving forward, that's when things started to grow. We started growing fast.

Before I knew it, we scaled to
100 agents. One hundred. And
I was doing everything—training,
managing, leading—while driving
almost an hour from my house to
the office every single day. I was tired.
Worn out. Running on faith, fumes,
and purpose. Here's the part people
don't see: *I didn't even fully know
the industry yet.* I wasn't the most
knowledgeable person in the room,
but I was the leader. I leaned on my
God-given ability to organize people,
communicate vision, and move with

confidence even when the outcome wasn't guaranteed.

We were everywhere. Car dealerships. Apartment complexes. Community spaces. Flat Fee was buzzing. That first season, I didn't make a lot of money, but I made a lot of noise. And sometimes, noise is leverage. Looking back, I can see it clearly now. The Most High didn't send everything at once. He sent what I needed, when I needed it. And as long as I trusted Him, He made room for me. It wasn't always easy. A lot of it didn't make sense at the time. But those moments weren't reasons to lose hope. They were reminders to keep the faith and keep pressing forward. Because if God gives you the idea, He will also make the provision for it. That belief carried me. And once I truly surrendered to that. Once I stayed willing and obedient, things began to shift. Slowly at first. Then all at once.

Leverage isn't always about what you have in your bank account. Sometimes, leverage is credit when cash is gone. Sometimes it's people who believe before proof exists. Sometimes it's the vision God gave you that nobody else can see yet. I didn't start with money. I started with what was already in my hands—work ethic, leadership, relationships, faith, and the willingness to move even while I was scared. That's leverage.

REFLECTION:

LEVERAGE

Take a breath and reflect on what's already in your hands. Many of us don't realize we were born with everything we need. We just need to tap into it. We may need to develop more, but it's already in us. All we have to do is be willing to believe and take the steps that are required. We have to develop confidence in our abilities and what has been placed in us.

Leverage isn't about waiting for permission. It's about recognizing value—especially in places you've overlooked.

Ask yourself:

What skills, experiences, or relationships am I underestimating?

_____
_____
_____
_____
_____
_____
_____
_____
_____
_____
_____
_____
_____
_____
_____

Where am I waiting for more instead of working with what I already have?

_____

_____

_____

_____

_____

_____

_____

_____

_____

_____

_____

_____

_____

_____

_____

_____

Who have I been comparing myself to instead of trusting my own path?

_____

_____

_____

_____

_____

_____

_____

_____

_____

_____

_____

_____

_____

_____

_____

_____

Sometimes the breakthrough isn't new resources. It's a new perspective. Everything you need to start isn't ahead of you. A lot of it is already behind you, waiting to be acknowledged.

Leverage requires honesty, humility, and courage. And once you see what you've been carrying all along, momentum follows.

CEO Mode Activated.

IMPLEMENTATION

When we got the opportunity to partner with Ace Check Cashing, that's when things really started to feel real. That partnership solidified something for me. It meant we weren't just an idea anymore. We were a real brand connected to a real entity. I'm not going to lie, it felt good. Seeing our signage, our people, our brand inside Ace meant something. It was one of those moments where you finally allow yourself to pause and acknowledge progress. One of those small milestones that helps you keep going. The fear was still there, but moments like that made it quieter. When you see things come into fruition, doubt starts to lose its grip.

The grand opening of Flat Fee was another one of those moments. It took something I had worked so hard for and made it tangible. I was surrounded by friends, family, and loved ones—people who had watched the grind, the late nights, the uncertainty, and now they were standing in the reality of it with me.

It's hard to put into words what that feels like. We didn't just open the doors to celebrate. We marketed the grand opening as an opportunity for new clients to actually come in and get their taxes done, *and people showed up*. We had agents there preparing tax returns. Business was happening in real time. We were all dressed in our Flat Fee gear. Everything I had envisioned was standing right in front of me. It wasn't a dream anymore. It wasn't theoretical. It was real.

For me, that day felt like crossing a finish line, even though I knew it was only the beginning. It felt like the moment where true entrepreneurship officially started. Something inside me settled. Like, *okay... you can do this*. And that feeling didn't mean the journey was over. It just meant I finally believed I was capable of seeing it through.

I remember the shift clearly. People reporting to me. People calling me "boss." Writing checks. Making decisions that impacted more than just my own life. And surprisingly, it felt natural.

Leadership wasn't something I had to learn from scratch. It was already in me. It was in alignment with the role I had played for years at the apartment complex. Long before I had the title, I was already helping run the ship. I was making decisions, solving problems, managing people, and keeping things moving. The only difference now was ownership. This time, the responsibility didn't come with a paycheck from someone else's company. It came with the weight and the freedom of building my own. And instead of feeling overwhelmed by that responsibility, I felt prepared for it. Because I had already been doing the work. Now I was just finally doing it for myself. That's when the hustle turned into a company. Now, don't get me wrong, it was busy. It was a lot of movement. Phones ringing. People training. Clients are coming in. Things are happening all at once. But somehow, in the middle of what looked like chaos to everybody else, I had peace. And I know where that peace came from.

God gave me the ability to manage. Not just people, pressure. Not just systems, but responsibility. He gave me the calm to make clear decisions even when there was a lot happening around me. I didn't panic. I didn't freeze. I didn't second-guess myself. Something in me just said, *This is what we're doing now. Let's get to it.*

CALL IT GRIT. CALL IT HUSTLE. CALL IT EXPERIENCE. WHATEVER IT WAS, IT HAD BEEN BRED INTO ME OVER YEARS OF SHOWING UP WHEN THINGS WERE UNCOMFORTABLE. AND NOW, ALL OF THAT WAS BEING ACTIVATED AT ONCE.

This is what implementation looks like. It's not perfect. It doesn't wait until you feel ready. It shows up when the doors open and people are standing there expecting you to lead. And I led.

REFLECTION:

IMPLEMENTATION

This is where things get real. Implementation doesn't wait until you feel ready. It shows up when movement becomes non-negotiable.

Ask yourself:

What idea have I been thinking about

but not acting on?

_____

_____

_____

_____

_____

_____

_____

_____

_____

_____

_____

_____

_____

_____

_____

_____

Where am I stuck in planning instead of doing?

_____
_____
_____
_____
_____
_____
_____
_____
_____
_____
_____
_____
_____
_____
_____
_____

If I took one imperfect step today, what would it be?

_____

_____

_____

_____

_____

_____

_____

_____

_____

_____

_____

_____

_____

_____

_____

_____

_____

Action doesn't eliminate fear. It just stops fear from being in control. Nothing moves forward while everything stays hypothetical.

Progress happens when intention meets execution. The moment you decide to move—messy, unsure, unpolished—is the moment things begin to shift.

CEO MODE ACTIVATED.

CONFIDENCE

The craziest part about Flat Fee is that I built it from nothing. I got it out of the mud. From scratch. And eventually, it became a six-figure brand. Flat Fee blessed me financially. It gave me stability. It worked. It was profitable. Predictable. Every year, I knew exactly what the numbers would look like. And yet, somewhere along the way, it began to lose its heart. The work became robotic. Redundant. Stale. What once felt purposeful turned into something I could do on autopilot. It no longer fulfilled me. That's when I understood the truth: Flat Fee was built in survival mode. And survival can only sustain you for so long. The shift didn't happen all at once. There was no dramatic turning point—just a gradual awareness that grew louder over time.

As my income changed, so did my environment. I found myself in rooms with people operating at a different level—people with access to information, resources, and opportunities I had never been exposed to before. Watching them changed me. I saw how they used tax income as a tool—funding investments, building businesses, expanding into other arenas. Taxes were simply the vehicle. For me, taxes had become the destination. And I knew I was meant for more. Still, I stayed longer than my passion did—because fear is convincing, and I didn't want to be poor again. I resisted the realization because the business worked. Walking away from something that produces income is scary, especially when you know what it's like to have nothing. But deep down, I knew this truth: *just because something works doesn't mean it's where you're supposed to stay.*

If I had stayed, I would have plateaued. I would have been comfortable but stifled. I would have burned out slowly, disconnected from my purpose, going through the motions instead of growing. The thrill was gone. And when the thrill is gone, momentum fades. What I was feeling wasn't boredom. It was expansion. Something in me wanted more than maintenance. More than predictability. More than profit. I wanted my work to mean something beyond me.

I wanted to serve. I wanted people who looked like me, who came from where I came from, to have access to the information and resources I once had to stumble into on my own. I didn't fully understand what that assignment was yet. I just knew I couldn't stay where I was. There were other people I needed to meet.

Other rooms I needed to enter. Other ways I needed to grow and other ways I needed to generate income. And staying focused solely on tax prep would have kept me content, but constrained. And I've never been called to live a constrained life. So I pivoted. I decided I no longer wanted to do tax prep. I wanted to teach it. I started offering tax software to other tax professionals and stepped into coaching and mentorship. I began helping EROs start, scale, and streamline six-figure tax firms because

I had already done it. And for the first time, I didn't have to guess if I was qualified. I knew what I was talking about.

That shift did something to me. Showing people how to build what I had built. Watching them go from confused to confident. Hearing their voices crack with gratitude. Seeing their tears when things finally clicked for them. That kind of confidence is different. It's one thing to know you can take nothing and make something. It's another thing to help someone else do it—and watch it change their life. That's when confidence stops being loud and starts being rooted. And that's when my perspective shifted again.

I wanted to give back in a bigger way. I wanted impact beyond business. So I started a nonprofit called Woke Money Movement. Financial literacy. Ownership. Information that we simply weren't given. I wanted to pour into the Black and Brown community because I was an example of what was possible. But here's the part people don't talk about. Even as the founder. Even as the connector. Even as the one curating the rooms, I sometimes felt like I didn't belong in them.

Woke Money exposed me to real-life millionaires. People opening doors I had never walked through before. And suddenly, imposter syndrome started creeping in. *Am I good enough to be here? Do I actually belong in this space?* And what made it complicated was this: I was the one bringing people together, but still questioning myself. That's when I learned something about confidence. Confidence doesn't mean fear disappears. It means you stop letting fear disqualify you. I started to realize something important. I wasn't in those rooms by accident. I wasn't building these spaces by mistake. And I hadn't just "gotten lucky." I had earned my seat, even if my journey didn't look like anyone else's.

For a long time, I questioned whether I belonged. I compared my path to people who had degrees, pedigrees, or polished backstories. But the truth is, confidence doesn't come from looking like everyone else. It comes from surviving what others never had to face and still showing up. And if you're reading this, I need you to hear this clearly:

YOU DON'T NEED PERMISSION TO BELONG. YOU DON'T NEED TO WAIT UNTIL YOUR STORY LOOKS CLEANER.

You don't need to minimize your journey to make others comfortable. If you're in the room, you earned it. If you're building something from scratch, it matters. If you're still standing after everything you've been through, that counts. Your path doesn't have to make sense to anyone else. It only has to make sense to you and align with who you're becoming. Confidence isn't about knowing everything. It's about trusting that what you've lived qualifies you. And once you stop shrinking, stop apologizing, and stop questioning whether you belong, that's when things really begin to shift. Because you don't stumble into purpose. You grow into it.

CONFIDENCE ISN'T ABOUT TITLES. IT'S ABOUT IMPACT. AND I FINALLY UNDERSTOOD MINE.

REFLECTION:

CONFIDENCE

Confidence isn't loud. It's built quietly through repetition, resilience, and results.

Ask yourself:

Where do I doubt myself even

though I've already proven my

ability?

_____
_____
_____
_____
_____
_____
_____
_____
_____
_____
_____
_____
_____
_____
_____
_____

What rooms do I enter questioning if I belong?

_____

_____

_____

_____

_____

_____

_____

_____

_____

_____

_____

_____

_____

_____

_____

_____

What version of confidence do I admire that I haven't allowed myself to step into yet?

_____

_____

_____

_____

_____

_____

_____

_____

_____

_____

_____

_____

_____

_____

_____

_____

Confidence grows when you stop asking for permission to be who you already are. You don't need validation to be qualified. You don't need titles to take up space. You belong where your work has taken you, even when your mind says otherwise. Stand in that truth.

CEO MODE ACTIVATED.

KEEP GOING

Being good at a lot of things can be both a blessing and a curse. On the surface, it sounds like an advantage. But when it comes to building a life and making money, it can actually create confusion. You don't always know what's driving you, whether it's passion, talent, opportunity, or survival. And when you're good at multiple things, deciding which direction to go in becomes harder than people realize. What happens is subtle. You start working on one thing, then drift to another. You get distracted. Not because you lack focus, but because you have too many options. Too many things you can do. And when you're known as the person who can figure things out, people lean on you. They rely on you. You become the go-to. The fixer. The one who can always make it work. That's where it gets dangerous. Because without realizing it, you start serving other people's needs instead of your own. You pour energy into their projects, their problems, their priorities —

while yours get pushed to the side. Add a giving heart to that equation, and it becomes a recipe for burnout.

I found myself working on their stuff and my stuff, constantly moving, constantly busy, but not always making progress. Just because you can do something doesn't mean you should. As entrepreneurs, our time has to be spent on money-making activities. But when you're good at everything, it's easy to mistake busyness for progress. You look productive. You feel needed.

But nothing is actually moving forward. And that's one of the most dangerous traps of being capable, confusing effectiveness with assignment. Because being good at something doesn't automatically make it your calling. And if you don't learn the difference, you can stay busy for years without ever truly advancing. And I learned that the hard way.

Woke Money started growing legs. Big legs. Building community, bringing people together, hosting events. That was a real passion for me. It felt good. It looked good. But the truth is, it didn't pay me. And that's where things get complicated. Perception is reality. When people see you hosting major events, pulling off big initiatives, and executing things flawlessly, they celebrate you. They assume you're thriving. They assume you're up. And they don't see the back end. They don't see you scraping things together. They don't see you on your last leg, still showing up strong. So you look like a hero, even when you're barely holding it together. That's especially true when you're doing things outside of the norm. Most people are part of the 99 percent. So when you move differently, think differently, build differently, you automatically look bigger than life. You get applauded just for daring to do something most people wouldn't even try. But applause doesn't pay bills. With Woke Money, that feeling came back, the same feeling I had during my production days. Red carpets.

Recognition. Praise. And once again, the math wasn't *mathing*. The bank account didn't match the optics. And that was scary.

Honestly, that season felt more dangerous than starting Flat Fee. At least with Flat Fee, there was structure. I knew if I did this many tax returns, I'd make this much money. There was a formula. With Woke Money, it was passion-driven, and passion alone doesn't keep the lights on. It was a beautiful initiative. It just wasn't aligned to support me financially. And when you're a full-time entrepreneur—no job, no side hustle, no safety net, your time has to produce revenue. That's a truth a lot of people don't like to talk about.

VISION NEEDS FUNDING. PASSION NEEDS STRUCTURE. WITHOUT BOTH, EVEN THE BEST IDEAS CAN PUSH YOU BACK INTO SURVIVAL MODE.

That's exactly what was happening to me. What Woke Money taught me was this: get the revenue solid first. Stabilize yourself before you start pouring into passion projects. Don't jump too quickly just because something feels good or looks impactful. Because impact without income will eventually cost you. And learning that lesson, as painful as it was, saved me from repeating the same cycle all over again. What happened next almost took me out.

Because my focus had shifted so heavily into Woke Money, my bread and butter—Flat Fee—began to slip. At the time, I didn't see it as neglect. I told myself I was expanding, evolving, building something bigger. But Flat Fee had always required proximity. Consistent mentoring. Thirty to forty clients at a time. That steady rhythm sustained everything. And without it, the foundation quietly weakened. A year passed before I fully faced it. I sat down with my bookkeeper, and she looked at me and said something I'll never forget: *"I don't even know how you paid your bills this year."* When we ran the numbers and the $200,000 loss stared back at me, imposter syndrome hit hard. My first reaction wasn't strategy. It wasn't solutions. It was doubt.

I started questioning everything. I wondered if all the success I'd had before was just luck. Maybe I had been in the right place at the right time. Maybe my blessings had run out. I began to doubt whether I was ever really that good at what I did. I took it hard. Depression settled in quietly and then all at once. I found myself confined to my bed for days at a time. I didn't want to get up. I didn't want to leave the house. I didn't want to go anywhere. I wasn't sleeping. I wasn't eating. Motivation was gone. And the scariest part was this: as an entrepreneur, I make money with my mind. When my mind went dark, my income followed. The loss didn't just hurt financially. It pushed me deeper into a hole mentally. And the deeper that hole got, the harder it felt to climb out.

I truly thought about quitting. I redid my résumé. I tried to convince myself that maybe entrepreneurship wasn't for me after all. I even applied for jobs. But when I got interviews, people would look at my background and say things like, *"You could run this company."* They didn't understand why I was even there. What they didn't see was how broken my confidence was.

In full transparency, there are only a handful of people who knew how bad it really got. Losing that much money stripped me of belief. I wasn't ashamed. I was confused. I didn't know how to pull myself out of it. And the truth is, most people couldn't help. A lot of people don't make close to $200,000 in a year, so they couldn't even fathom what that kind of loss feels like. There wasn't much anyone could say. What carried me through that season was God. Prayer. And a few friends who didn't understand the numbers but loved me anyway. They sat with me. They checked on me. They reminded me I wasn't alone, and they held hope for me when I couldn't hold it myself.

Some days, I didn't believe things would get better. I just kept showing up anyway. I prayed when I didn't have words. I leaned on faith when logic failed me. And slowly, piece by piece, God pulled me out. Sometimes it takes God Himself to lift you from a place you can't climb out of on your own. And when there's purpose in your life, He won't leave you there.

That season almost broke me. But it didn't. That's something nobody really prepares you for. Because when you're part of the one percent—the people who make money with their own two hands—most people around you don't understand your pressure. Not because they don't care, but because they can't relate. Support only goes so far when comprehension isn't there. That's why faith mattered. For me, it was staying connected to the Most High.

Believing that I wasn't abandoned.

Believing that nothing I was going through was wasted. I stopped calling it a loss and started calling it a lesson. Because every lesson prepares you for the next level if you keep going.

It took me nearly a year and a half to crawl out of that financial hole. And truthfully, I'm still rebuilding in some areas.

But I didn't stop.
I didn't quit.

Flat Fee is still here.

Still standing.

Still moving.

And now, new initiatives are forming. Things I'll talk about later. Maybe even in another book.

But the point is this.

Success doesn't come from never falling. It comes from refusing to stay down.

If you're in a season where things don't make sense... If you're talented but overwhelmed... If you're carrying vision with no validation yet...*Keep going.*

That's CEO mode. Not the highlights. Not the applause. *The stay.*

REFLECTION:

KEEP GOING

This one matters most. Because sometimes staying matters more than starting.

Ask yourself:

What has made me want to quit more

than once?

_____

_____

_____

_____

_____

_____

_____

_____

_____

_____

_____

_____

_____

_____

_____

_____

What season tested me in ways no one else could see?

_____

_____

_____

_____

_____

_____

_____

_____

_____

_____

_____

_____

_____

_____

_____

_____

_____

If I kept going anyway, what could be

possible on the other side?

_____
_____
_____
_____
_____
_____
_____
_____
_____
_____
_____
_____
_____
_____
_____

There will be moments where motivation disappears. Where progress slows. Where results don't match effort. This is where most people stop. But persistence isn't about feeling strong. It's about choosing not to surrender. Every lesson you survive sharpens you for what's next. You didn't come this far to turn around now.

Keep going.

Once it clicks, there's no going back.
CEO MODE ACTIVATED.

A LETTER TO THE READER

If you made it this far, I just want to say thank you. Thank you for reading my story. Thank you for sitting with it. Thank you for allowing me to be honest, vulnerable, and real with you.

This book was personal. It was my first. And in many ways, writing it felt like letting you into rooms of my life that most people never see.

By reading it, you became part of my journey. My hope from the very beginning was never just to motivate you, but to *stand with you*. To be the voice I needed when I was trying to figure it out. To be the reminder that you're not crazy for wanting more — and you're not alone in the process of becoming it.

If this book spoke to you, that's not by accident. And if you feel like you need guidance, structure, or accountability along your journey, I want you to know this: you don't have to do it alone.

If you need a Ms Cat in your life—a coach, an accountability partner, and a teacher, stay connected with me.

You can find me:
@connectwithmscat on all socials and at www.connectwithmscat.com

This won't be my last book and this won't be the last time you hear from me. But wherever this journey takes you next, I hope you move forward with confidence, intention, and belief in what's possible for you.

Until next time,

Ms Cat